Apple's new Neighbors

Written and Illustrated by:
Bethany & Olivia Moy

To:
Ava,
Leah,
and
Allie ♡

'16

Olivia L Moy
Bethany L Moy

In Loving Memory of

Isabel

Apple

Elisa

In a BIG, BIG city,
In a house large and posh...

APPLE'S PLACE

2

3

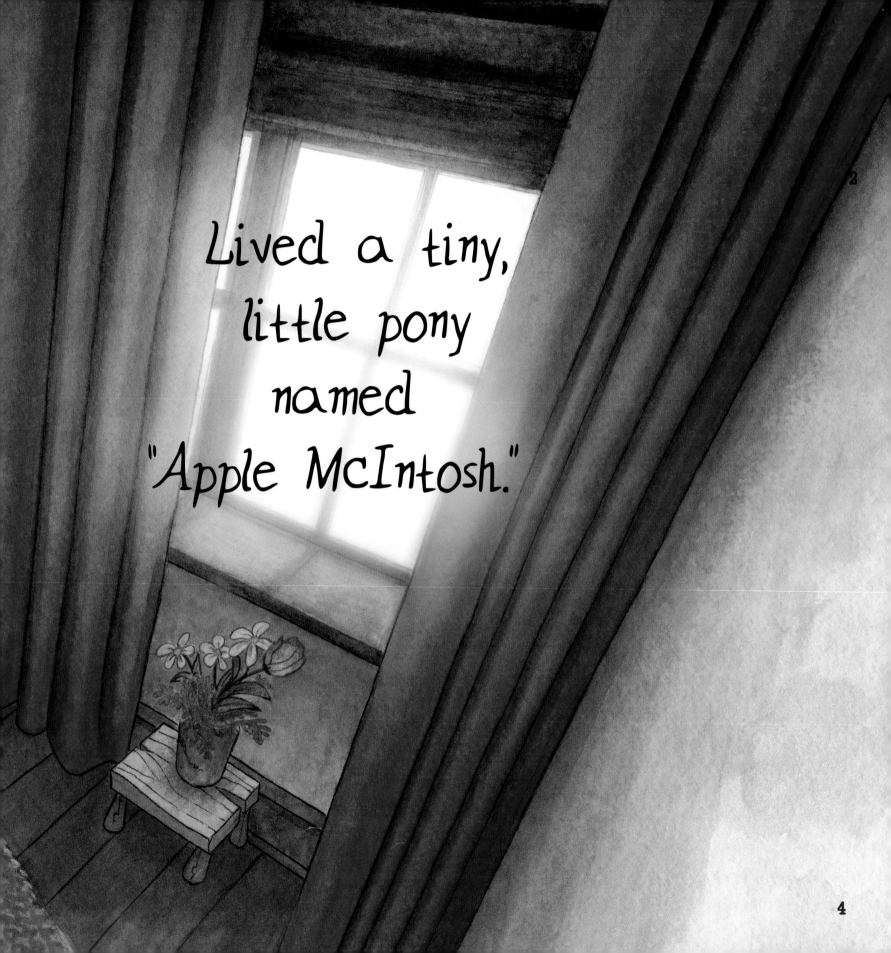

Lived a tiny,
little pony
named
"Apple McIntosh."

She was very, very lonely.

Her friend moved far away,

And someone else was coming

To that empty house to stay.

I am very, very lonely;
And very, very shy.
I will never make new friends,
But stay here by and by!

At that,
She heard
A noise!

9

11

MOVE >>>

Her new neighbors
Were moving into
That empty house
Next door.

But scared
and shy,
She turned
away--
Just as
she
heard a

13

14

And this, madam, is true:
A FRIEND we'd like to make...
So if a friend you'd like us as,
Good memories we'll make!

Now Apple's lonely times
Have finally gone away!
Because of her new friends,
FOREVER TOGETHER
They'll stay!

Our Inspiration for Creating "Apple's New Neighbors"

Here are some pictures of the "real" Apple and her two goat neighbors: Isabel and Elisa

Apple

Bethany & Isabel

Olivia & Elisa

About the Authors

Bethany and Olivia Moy formed their love of drawing when they could first hold crayons. Since then, the sisters have passionately pursued art. Their artistic journey eventually lead them to study Traditional Animation and Visual Development at the Academy of Art University. In December of 2014, they graduated with a BFA in Classical Animation. *Apple's New Neighbors* is their first published children's book.

The inspiration for this book came from their pets: an old Shetland pony named Apple, and two sweet Pygmy goat sisters named Isabel and Elisa. Even though Apple, Isabel, and Elisa have passed away, their friendship, love, and memories will always live in Bethany and Olivia's hearts.

The Moy sisters currently reside in rural Pennsylvania, where they work daily to create animated videos and illustrations for their new company, The *Little Sisters Studio.*